Saltwater Aquariums

Learn How to Properly Set Up Your Tank and Make Your Fish Thrive

By Anthony Daniels

Table of Contents

Introduction

If you are planning to get your own saltwater aquarium, there are very specific steps you should follow in setting it up. Always keep in mind that you are dealing with saltwater fish here.

This means that all of the fish you put into the tank have specific needs. You don't take care of them the way you would take care of freshwater fish.

Many people often make the wrong assumption that all you need to do is dump seawater into the tank and you are good to go. No, it doesn't work that way.

Taking care of saltwater fish needs a little bit of extra attention and work compared to taking care of their freshwater counterparts.

In this book, I am going to guide you through the exact process on how to set up your saltwater tank and how you can make sure that all of your fish are well-taken care of. There's a ton of information that you need to digest.

I broke this information down into actionable steps so you can easily understand and implement them.

Setting up and maintaining a healthy saltwater aquarium is an art in itself. If you have no idea what you are doing, your fish can die from a variety of problems.

You may be using the wrong type of water. You may be using inappropriate tank equipment. You may be feeding your fish the wrong food. And so on and so forth.

There's also the fact that every type of saltwater fish or marine organism that you put into the tank often needs specific care. Think of it as similar to maintaining a zoo.

The needs of zebras are different from the needs of savannah lions. In the same sense, the butterfly fish may have different needs compared to the watchman goby.

You have to be aware of these discrepancies in needs and maintenance before you start dumping marine organisms into your tank.

Compatibility is another very important factor that you must always keep in mind. Using our earlier analogy, if you are running a zoo, you don't put the zebras and the lions in the same cage.

They don't belong together. In short, they are incompatible. The same principle applies to maintain a saltwater aquarium.

There are certain species of saltwater fish or marine organisms that are simply not compatible. This is a simple fact that a lot of beginners often take for granted. Don't make that mistake.

What I'm trying to say here is that paying attention to details is very important when it comes to setting up and maintaining a saltwater tank. This is why I've written this book to help anyone who has plans of setting up his own saltwater aquarium.

This book contains every piece of information that you need to get started. So let's dig in, shall we?

Before we get into the nitty gritty of the book please consdier leaving a review if you enjoy it. Even just a few words will help other people know if the book is right for them.

Many thanks in advance!

Chapter One: The Differences between a Saltwater Tank and a Freshwater Tank

Before anything else, it's very important that you understand the differences between a saltwater tank and a freshwater tank. It's a no-brainer but there are still people out there who think that maintaining a saltwater tank is the same as maintaining a freshwater tank.

They end up killing most of if not all of their fish in the process. Maintaining a saltwater tank is much more complicated, to say the least. Let's take a quick look into some of the main differences in setting up a saltwater tank compared to a freshwater tank.

Initial Setup

Generally speaking, setting up a saltwater tank is more difficult and more expensive. It costs more because you have to regularly purchase salt to mix into the water in order to make the aquarium habitable for marine organisms.

Purchasing salt is not a major expense but it's something that you must always monitor to ensure that proper salinity is maintained inside the tank.

Minor fluctuations in salinity are alright but large fluctuations are never acceptable. Huge swings in salinity can cause extreme stress to the creatures inside the tank.

Improper salinity is one of the most common reasons why saltwater fish die inside their tanks. Salinity is not something you would be concerned about if you owned a freshwater fish tank.

Time Spent in Monitoring the Tank

Saltwater fish are much more sensitive compared to their freshwater counterparts. Saltwater fish require more care and attention.

You are going to spend more time monitoring the conditions of the tank and the creatures inside it. There are a lot of factors that you must monitor such as the alkalinity and pH levels in the water.

These water parameters have to be at the proper levels if you want your fish to live and stay healthy. You also have to modulate these levels using buffers or additives if necessary.

Availability of Fish

It is more difficult to find saltwater fish compared to freshwater fish. If you are to visit a fish store, only a small percentage of the fish you see there are saltwater fish.

They are much harder to find. Saltwater fish aren't easily accessible because they are primarily collected in the wild.

Only a few hundred species of marine fish can be successfully bred in captivity. Compare this to the fact that 95% of freshwater fish can be bred in captivity.

The main point here is that since saltwater fish have to be caught in the wild before being sold to fish stores, they are usually more expensive and a lot harder to find.

The Risks Involved

Maintaining a saltwater aquarium is riskier in the sense that there are more reasons why your fish would die out. Fish of the freshwater variety are simply tougher and are more capable of adapting to harsh environments.

Saltwater fish, on the other hand, are often too sensitive. Slight changes in the water's temperature, salinity, or pH levels can pose a serious danger to the health of the fish.

This is why these factors have to be regularly monitored and monitoring these factors takes a bit of time.

Maintaining a Stable and Ideal Environment

Just think about it. Saltwater environments are much more complicated compared to freshwater environments. It then follows that it is going to be much harder to maintain a stable and ideal environment in a saltwater tank.

Keep in mind that with a saltwater aquarium, you are attempting to recreate what a normal sea community looks like. This means that the water has to be right.

The corals have to be the proper species. The sand has to be of the right kind.

And so on and so forth. In short, it can be rather complicated. Compare that to the process of setting up a freshwater tank wherein you can just dump water and gravel in the tank and you are good to go.

Ornamental Invertebrates Consideration

Saltwater tanks may require ornamental invertebrates such as anemones and corals in order for certain saltwater fish species to thrive. These organisms are very common in natural environments.

In many ways, certain saltwater fish need these invertebrates to thrive. There exists a mutual relationship among these sea creatures.

You take one away and the other might not do as good. For example when you think of a clownfish what do you think of? Probably an anemone right? As it turns out a clownfish doesn't have to have an anemone, but an anemone will give the clownfish a place in the tank where it can go and feel safe.

The good news is that fish stores are getting better and smarter in pairing the right saltwater fish species with the right sea invertebrates. So if you're unsure of exactly what can go together, you should be able to get the help you need at the store.

Be that as it may, I suggest that you do your own in-depth research into the matter especially if you are targeting a specific species of saltwater fish for your tank.

The main takeaway here is that setting up and maintaining a saltwater tank is more difficult, more expensive, and has more requirements compared to setting up and maintaining a freshwater tank.

With that being said, you need to prepare in advance. Maintaining a saltwater tank is going to take a lot of your time and effort.

This is especially true if you live in an area that is a good distance away from something such as a pet store because resources might not be easily accessible.

Chapter Two: How to Properly Set Up a Saltwater Tank

In this chapter, I am going to show you the exact steps on how to properly set up your own saltwater aquarium. If it's your first time to set up a saltwater tank, I highly recommend that you start with a simple one.

Your initial focus should be on learning everything that you can about setting up and maintaining the tank. Only when you have gathered enough knowledge and experience that you should consider getting a much more complicated saltwater aquarium.

Here are the main steps in setting up a saltwater tank:

Step 1: Decide if you are going to create a fish only tank or a reef tank.

There is a huge difference between the two. A fish-only tank is very simple in the sense that it only contains the fish, live rock, and possibly a good amount of sand.

Fish-only tanks are easy to build and set up. On the other hand, a reef tank is one that is complete with corals, sea anemones, even transplanted seaweeds, and other necessary marine organisms.

What some people do is start with a fish-only tank then slowly upgrade it to a reef tank.

For example, you begin with a pretty basic saltwater tank that only contains a few fish, some rocks, and sand. Over time, you slowly introduce new fish, corals, sea anemones, sea invertebrates, and other sea creatures into the tank.

This slow-building strategy is advisable if you are setting up a really huge tank. Even if you don't think you want a big tank, it might be a good idea to go ahead and buy a larger tank size than you initially want.

The reason for this is later on down the line, you might get interested in a certain fish species or coral and not have the necessary room to accommodate for what you want to add. If you have a bigger tank size than it won't be an issue.

However, if you start off with a smaller tank, then you won't be able to upgrade the size once everything is set up.

The slow-building strategy is also a good way to learn more about the needs and wants of your saltwater fish. As you introduce more fish into the tank, you get to observe how they adapt to the new environment. This will help you in taking better care of the tank and all the organisms that live inside it.

Step 2: Decide what your tank would look like.

You have two choices. You can either build the tank from scratch or you can purchase a ready-made tank.

I would not recommend the first option if you know nothing about how tanks work and how these are maintained. I always advise new tank owners to purchase ready-made tanks.

Most fish stores also sell tanks in various sizes, shapes, and designs. Some of them even offer customized designs.

You can have a tank customized depending on your personal preferences.

When deciding on the look of your tank, you must consider the location where you plan on installing it. It should be in a location that is clean and free from harmful particles that might make their way into the tank.

Always seek advice from the person you are buying the tank from. The owner or the keeper of a fish supplies store should be able to provide you with the information you are looking for. Don't be afraid to ask for tips and advice.

Step 3: Choose your tank stand and hood.

The majority of saltwater tanks come with a stand and a hood. The stand is the platform which acts as the support for the framework of the tank.

The stand serves several purposes. Firstly, it provides structural support for the tank.

Secondly, it elevates the tank so that it doesn't sit directly on the floor. And thirdly, if your stand has wheels it makes it so much easier to move the tank around should you ever decide to move it.

Step 4: Start writing a tank log book.

You may be wondering why you need a log book. Well, it's mostly for tracking and monitoring reasons.

The logbook serves as a record of all the things you do to the tank and the fish and creatures that you put in it. It's important to keep a detailed record of everything that you do with your tank.

From the equipment you use to the critters that you put inside, these have to be recorded for future reference. You can use a traditional notebook or record book.

Or you can use one of the freeware and shareware logbooks that are available online. Some of these online logbooks come in the form of a mobile app. Some are free to download and some require a subscription.

Step 5: Get a biological filtration system.

In order for a saltwater aquarium to function properly, it must have what is referred to as a biological filter. The occupants of your tank produce all sorts of toxic wastes like ammonia, nitrates, and nitrites.

If these build up inside your tank, they can easily kill off the organisms inside it one by one. To deal with this problem, you need a biological filtration system.

What the biological filter does is convert the toxic wastes into harmless compounds and elements. The filter accomplishes this by using the bacteria that are naturally found in the oceans to process the wastes.

Some shops sell saltwater tanks with built-in filtration systems and some don't. With that said, you have to be more scrutinizing about the tank you are going to buy.

There is what is referred to in the industry as the nitrogen cycle. I will discuss this in more detail in an upcoming chapter but let me provide you with a quick overview of how the cycle works.

Saltwater fish give off a toxin called ammonia in their waste. The bacteria in the filter breaks down the ammonia and converts them into nitrite which is still toxic and can harm your fish.

The nitrites will eventually get broken down into nitrates which are only toxic in large amounts. However, the nitrates in your tank will still accumulate in the water but it can no longer be broken down.

Therefore the best way to get rid of it is to remove some of the water, clean the tank, and replace the water on a regular basis. That's how the nitrogen cycle goes.

There are other filtration methods aside from biological filtration. These will be further discussed in another chapter.

Several factors come into consideration when it comes to choosing the best filtration system for your saltwater tank. There are questions you need to ask yourself.

Are you going to use sumps? Are you going to use under gravel filters?

Are you going to use wet and dry trickle filters? Or would you prefer using canister filters? As I've mentioned, these will be discussed in further detail in another chapter.

Step 6: Choose the right water for the tank.

It's a no-brainer that tap water is never okay to use in a marine aquarium. Still, many people make such a dangerous mistake.

This is especially true in urban centers wherein tap water is often mixed with a number of chemicals that can be very toxic to marine organisms and invertebrates. Such chemicals include fluoride, chlorine, chloramine, phosphate, nitrate, and copper. All of these are toxic to sea creatures.

So if you can't use tap water, what kind of water should you use? So far, most experienced fish tank owners would recommend reverse osmosis de-ionized water.

This is often referred to in the industry as RO water. Where can you find this type of water? It's usually sold in local aquarium stores.

Sometimes, you can even find them in grocery stores. But if you don't have access to RO water, you can always use distilled water. But nothing can beat the quality of RO water.

I highly recommend that you invest in an RO/DI filter unit. This is basically a filtration system that comes with a reverse osmosis filter membrane and several filter canisters which include a de-ionization filter (DI).

An RO/DI filter is not that expensive. You can purchase a high-quality unit for as low as $150.

Getting a filter unit will be much more convenient compared to carrying buckets or bags of water from the local aquarium store.

You should also consider purchasing a total dissolved solids (TDS) meter along with the filter unit. What this meter does is monitor and check the quality of the water.

This way, you will be able to know if it's time to change the water and clean the tank. Some brands of RO/DI filter units come with their own TDS meters so you should watch out for this.

Don't forget to ask the storekeeper if the filter unit comes with a TDS meter.

Removing and replacing the water in your saltwater tank can be a lot of work. You should get a large plastic trash can with wheels and use it as storage for ready-made saltwater that you can put in your tank when you need to do a water change.

Step 7: Choose the proper substrate for your saltwater aquarium.

If you don't already know, the substrate is composed of the materials that you are going to put on the bottom of the tank.

The good news is that you have several options when it comes to the substrate.

Marine aquariums usually make use of crushed coral, sand, or a combination of both materials. For saltwater tanks, the best substrates are the ones that are high in calcium.

This is why crushed coral is very popular among aquarium owners. Another popular option is a type of fine sand called aragonite.

You can also make use of live sand as substrate. What makes live sand unique is that it is cultured in the ocean and it contains a good amount of naturally-occurring bacteria that are beneficial to the occupants of the tank.

Live sand can play an important role in keeping the water clean.

The substrate has quite a few functions that are very important to the overall appearance and health of the tank. First and foremost, the substrate is decorative since it gives the tank its natural look.

Imagine a tank which contains no substrate at the bottom. It's really ugly and barren looking.

The substrate is not just decorative, it can also be a part of the tank's biological filtration system. It can also be home to tiny sand-dwelling critters that play an important role in the maintenance of the tank.

Step 8: Choose the proper types of salts that you are going to mix into your tank.

Choosing the right type of salt is very important especially if you are planning to set up a reef tank. There are various brands of sea salts being sold out there.

I suggest that you talk with the aquarium shopkeeper and ask what his recommendations would be depending on the type and size of saltwater tank you plan on building.

You should also inform him about the species of fish that you are going to put into the tank. With the knowledge and background that they usually have, aquarium shopkeepers should be able to provide you with practical suggestions with regards to the types of sea salts that you might need to use.

Step 9: Set up the saltwater tank's lighting fixtures.

Just like most living and moving organisms, marine fish recognize their days and their nights. This is why it's very important that you keep the tank's lighting fixtures in order.

There should be a regular cycle of light each day because this is required for the overall well-being of the marine creatures. What you need to do is set up an accurate light timer that will automatically turn your lights on and off so that the tank gets a consistent cycle of light and darkness.

The majority of experts recommend that the saltwater tank should get between ten to twelve hours of light per day. That's consistent with the amount of light that marine creatures get in their wild and natural environments.

You have to maintain this cycle of eight to ten hours because if the numbers fluctuate too often, you can cause undue stress to the fish. In other words, proper lighting is crucial to the health and survival of every fish and marine critter that you place inside the tank.

Having the proper lighting is even more critical if you are putting live corals into the tank. Most coral species need light to process and make food.

This may also apply to other organisms you might have inside the tank. Without enough lighting, the health of the marine creatures will slowly deteriorate to the point that they start dying out.

You have several options when it comes to tank lighting. Your main choices include fluorescent lights, metal halide lights, and LED (light emitting diodes) lights.

Go through the pros and cons of each of these types of lights so that you can come up with a more informed decision.

Step 10: Stock the saltwater tank with the right fish species and marine critters.

Before you stock your tank with expensive fish or invertebrates, make sure all of your tank's levels are okay. Make sure the salinity, pH, ammonia, nitrite, and nitrate levels are all in order.

Most pet stores will test your water levels for free if you bring in a sample from your tank. They can use a small strip to test for most of these things.

However, to test for the salinity a larger sample will be needed. Make sure you bring 1-2 cups worth of your water to the store.

After doing water tests and making sure that everything is in order, it's time to stock the aquarium with real living saltwater fish. Fish aren't the only organism you can put inside the tank.

You can also consider putting critters like crabs and snails in the tank as well. They will be able to help with tank maintenance, they're cheap, and they won't require a lot of upkeep.

Most aquarium retailers offer these critters and organisms for sale. You can even purchase them online if they are not available at any aquarium store near you.

Don't forget to examine every fish you purchase especially if you are buying more expensive fish. Most of the vibrant-colored saltwater fish that aquarists enjoy are not exactly cheap.

And don't forget the fact that they are usually more sensitive compared to their freshwater counterparts.

One of the signs that something is wrong with a fish is if it has some markings on it like bruises or white spots. Their eyes should also be clear and not plain white.

Even better, try asking one of the store's staff to try feeding the fish. This is to make sure that they are healthy and eating.

It's a very common problem among fish buyers that they purchase fish that simply refuse to eat when they bring them home. I highly suggest that when you go to the aquarium store to purchase fish, you should bring someone with you who is knowledgeable and experienced about saltwater fish and their needs.

If that's not possible, then look for pictures online as to exactly what certain illnesses look like so you know exactly what to watch out for. And don't worry common fish illnesses will be covered in depth in chapter 7 if you're unsure of what to search for.

There are also factors you must consider when buying corals for your tank. The general rule when buying live corals is that you should always choose a specimen with fully open polyps.

This means that the corals are healthy and functioning properly. Furthermore, you should look for dead spots in the bodies of the corals.

If there are dead spots, don't buy them. These spots will usually get worse when you bring the corals home.

Every organism you put inside your tank should be inspected closely. Make sure that they are not diseased because one single diseased organism can spread its illness to the others inside the tank.

The health of every species is crucial to the health of the other species. For instance, a diseased snail can contaminate the tank and pose health dangers to the fish and other critters like crabs.

Don't worry though, I'll go over common fish illnesses to look out for in a later chapter.

After bringing the fish and critters home, don't dump them immediately into your tank. They have to be acclimated first to make sure that the new environment won't cause stress or harm.

Marine creatures are just like other organisms. If you suddenly take them to a whole new environment, they might not be able to adapt.

This is why it's important to acclimatize them first before you start putting them inside your tank.

Here's what you need to do for acclimatization. Put the fish you bought inside a clean bucket with the water that's in the bag with the fish.

Let them stay inside the bucket for several minutes. You then get water from your aquarium and slowly add the water into the bucket.

Do this slowly by using a cup or a siphoning hose. Gradually add more aquarium water into the bucket until the water in the bucket is three times more than the water that originally came with the fish.

Adding the water could take you between fifteen and thirty minutes.

Let the fish stay in the bucket for a few minutes. If you notice that the fish aren't having problems with the new water, you can slowly transfer them into the tank.

Use a soft net to transfer the fish. Some people make the mistake of pouring the bucket into the aquarium.

This isn't a good idea because you don't know what other critters or chemicals might be present in the original water that you brought from the aquarium store.

Step 11: Watch the fish and critters closely for the next few days if they are able to adapt to the new aquarium.

The first few days after the transfer are the most crucial days for adaptation and acclimatization. Some fish might get stressed by the new environment.

They may feel cramped because of the enclosure. Some may refuse to eat.

It's possible that some will die. These are risks that you must expect when transferring saltwater fish from one aquarium to another.

Another important thing you should pay attention to is the way the fish interact with each other. Are they constantly fighting each other?

Are they bickering over food even though there's more than enough for everyone? Are some fish aggressive while others seem tame and unresponsive?

If you notice any of these things, then something is possibly wrong. Consult with the people at the aquarium store where you bought the fish.

Ask them if the behavior is normal or if such behavior will go away with the passage of time.

These are the basic steps in properly setting up a saltwater tank. Make sure that you diligently follow them if you want to set up a healthy environment for your fish.

Be patient. Don't rush because as we have mentioned quite a few times already, saltwater fish are sensitive and it takes them more time to adapt to a new environment compared to freshwater fish.

Chapter Three: The Nitrogen Cycle and Its Importance in a Saltwater Tank

We touched on the nitrogen cycle a little bit in a previous chapter but it needs to be explained further because it plays a very important role in the maintenance of a saltwater tank (or a freshwater tank for that matter).

It's the most important thing you should know in making sure that the water in your saltwater tank is conducive to your fish's survival and health.

It can be disastrous to all the creatures in your tank for you to have no idea about the nitrogen cycle.

The nitrogen cycle is essentially a chain reaction within the water in the tank. In each reaction, a new type of bacteria is produced.

The new bacteria consumes the previous bacteria and in turn produce yet another form of bacteria. This cycle repeats itself over and over again inside the tank.

The three main components in the chain reaction are ammonia, nitrite, and nitrate.
In general, a nitrogen cycle takes about thirty (30) days. However, this is not an exact time frame because the nitrogen cycle depends on various factors that are unique to the tank.

For example, the size of the tank, the number of fish in it, and the presence of other marine creatures affect the completion of the nitrogen cycle.

Here are the three phases in a nitrogen cycle:

Phase 1 (Ammonia): This is the first component that is needed for the chain reaction to occur. The nitrogen cycle starts when ammonia begins to accumulate inside the tank.

Ammonia comes from the waste, excess food, and other decaying organic matter in the tank. High levels of ammonia in the water can be fatal to fish and other marine creatures.

Phase 2 (Nitrite): Approximately ten days into the cycle, the bacteria will convert from toxic ammonia into nitrite and build up inside the tank. The level of nitrite will continue to increase and then start to drop off at about three from when the cycle started.

The level should fall thereafter to zero ppm. Nitrite is toxic as well and can kill fish if the levels are too high.

Phase 3 (Nitrate): Nitrates are produced by the third and final nitrifying bacteria in the chain reaction. You should be able to tell if the nitrogen cycle has reached this final stage in the process if nitrate readings in the tank begin to significantly increase.

Why is it important for any aquarium owner to be aware of the nitrogen cycle? The answer is very simple.

The nitrogen cycle is a chemical process that makes the water livable for fish. Without the cycle, fish will get sick and eventually die.

The nitrogen cycle is the most important process in controlling a closed aquatic environment. It's necessary because the water is stuck in an enclosure, unlike the sea where saltwater freely moves around.

Not only is the nitrogen cycle a water purification process, but it's also a source of primary food production. No one should start an aquarium without understanding first how the nitrogen cycle works.

There are two main ways on how you can manually encourage the nitrogen cycle in your tank. One, you can directly add measured amounts of ammonia into the water.

And two, you can accomplish it by putting a few hardy species of saltwater fish that will produce the ammonia for you. You can start the cycling process with or without fish.

Most aquarium owners jumpstart the nitrogen cycle on a new tank through fishless cycling. This is also what I would recommend because it's less risky.

In fishless cycling, what you do is add fish food to the tank. A few days would go by and the food starts to decompose.

You should monitor the water for signs of ammonia development. The ammonia levels should be at about 3 ppm.

If this level drops, try adding more food into the water. In a week or so, test the water for nitrites.

If you get a positive reading, this means that the nitrogen cycle has started. The cycling process can take six to eight weeks.

The bottom line here is that you must understand how the nitrogen cycle works and how you can jumpstart it. As I said before, it's the most important process in controlling a closed aquatic environment.

Without proper cycling, the fish and all the creatures inside the tank will be exposed to all sorts of risks and diseases. That's why it's important to not get super expensive fish right off the bat.

You definitely want to make your tank is fully cycled before putting your prized $200 fish in the tank. If you're going to cycle your tank using fish start off with something hardy and inexpensive like a damselfish.

Are you enjoying this book so far? If so, I'd love it if you considered leaving a review. The feedback would be greatly appreciated and it'll help me make better content for readers like you in the future!

Chapter Four: Choosing the Right Fish for Your Saltwater Tank

A very common mistake among beginners is that they put the wrong species of fish together in the same tank. Just because it's a saltwater tank, that does not mean you can put any species of saltwater fish in it.

There are a lot of saltwater fish that can't live and survive alongside each other. Some are predators and some are prey.

You have to be careful in putting several species of saltwater fish in the same tank. Think of the tank like a zoo as I mentioned earlier.

You don't put the lions and the zebras in the same steel cage.

The first piece of advice I would like to give you with regards to this matter is that you should already have an idea of the species of the fish that you are going to use before you even start looking for a tank. This is for the simple reason that the survival of a fish depends a lot on the size and features of the tank.

Some species need a lot of room to swim which means you are going to need a larger tank. On the other hand, some species can survive even within a small and congested tank.

With that out of the way, let's go back to choosing the right fish for your saltwater tank. There are various factors that you must take into account when looking into your options.

If you know of someone who has experience buying and taking care of saltwater fish, I suggest that you bring him/her along when you go shopping for fish. The advice he/she provides you with will be very helpful in making sure that you get the right fish.

If you are a complete beginner, here are some of the best saltwater fish species I would suggest that you get. I recommend these because they are appropriate for starters.

They look good because of their bright and vibrant colors. They are easier to take care. And they tend to be tougher which basically means they have a better chance of surviving in a brand new environment.

Coral Beauty Angelfish– They eat almost anything so they're easier to feed.
Butterfly Fish– There are more than one hundred species of them so they are easy to find.
Watchman Goby– They can live peacefully with most species of saltwater fish.
Tangs- Very popular fish among aquarists thanks to their bright colors
Talbot's Damsel– One of the hardiest fish species out there.
Firefish– They are pretty easygoing and get along well with other fish.
Chalk Bass– They are super tough because they tend to be resistant to illnesses and water changes.
Wrasses– They don't cause much trouble because they get along well with most other fishes.
Dottyback– Hardy and tough, they don't succumb that easily to illnesses.
Blennys– Their serene and peaceful qualities allow them to live peacefully with other marine organisms in the tank.

I know that this is a rather short list of fish recommendations but I made it that way so that you can start with less on your plate. Choosing from dozens of fish species can be very confusing and frustrating.

That's why I want you to start with these ten species. They are known for their hardiness, vibrancy, and non-aggressive attitudes.

Choose the ones that catch your fancy. Taking care of these species is going to teach you a ton of lessons about maintaining a saltwater aquarium.

You will get a lot of valuable experience in the process. If you think you are ready, you can slowly add more advanced fish species in your tank.

A Quick Note on Fish Compatibility

Fish compatibility is a serious matter and it requires in-depth reading. The general rule is that you shouldn't put aggressive fish species together.

Also, you shouldn't put fish with predatory tendencies with other fish that are often considered as prey. Covering the compatibility of each and every fish species is beyond the scope of this book.

Therefore if you have specific questions about the compatibility of a certain fish, be sure to search for it online. With that being said here are some common community fish that are not aggressive if you're not sure where to start:

- Gobies
- Pajama Cardinals
- Coral Beauty Angelfish
- Royal Gramma
- Ocellaris
- Clownfish (this is the common orange and white clownfish)
- Chalk Bass
- Lawnmower Blennies

As a final recommendation if you want something you can easily reference you can search for a compatibility chart online.

This will make things much simpler than having to search online every time you want to see if a certain fish is compatible with another.

Chapter Five: Tips on Feeding Your Saltwater Fish

Saltwater fish are very sensitive creatures. I've said that several times but it's worth saying it again because a lot of new aquarium owners tend to take that fact for granted.

They end up killing their fish by feeding it the wrong fish food. In this chapter, I am going to provide you with a quick guide on how you should feed your saltwater fish.

Do your research on what to feed to a particular species of fish before you have the fish purchased and transferred to your saltwater aquarium. Don't make the mistake of purchasing the fish before trying to determine what kind of food it eats.

You should be ready with the food packs the moment the fish is placed inside the aquarium. The main reason for this is because certain species require live food.

If you don't have easy access to be able to purchase live food, then that particular fish isn't going to be a good fit for you.

The first thing you want to consider is the natural diets of the species of fish inside your tank. Are they carnivores, herbivores, or omnivores? Your goal is to replicate these natural diets as accurately as possible.

If the fish eats mostly algae in its natural environment, then it follows that you should be feeding it algae unless you can purchase processed fish food that can serve as a complete alternative.

Create a list of all the possible food you can give to every species of fish inside your tank. I highly suggest that you create an information table for this list, print it out, and have it posted near the aquarium.

This enables you to familiarize yourself with all the food alternatives. It also makes it easier to make a list of which items you should buy next from the pet store.

Always read the labels and instructions in a package of prepared fish food before you purchase it. There are usually instructions about which species you should feed it to, how much you should use in a feeding session, and how often you should feed the fish.

Feed your fish with a variety of food. Don't just rely on one or two types of fish food.

In their natural environment, saltwater fish have dozens of food items to choose from. With that being said, it makes sense to feed them a variety of foods in their enclosure.

Try to rotate as many different items as you can to ensure that your fish get all the essential nutrients they need. And don't be afraid to ask the pet store owner about his suggestions on what you should feed to your saltwater fish.

How much and how often should you feed your saltwater fish? There is no single answer to this question because feeding requirements vary from species to species.

However, it's always preferable to feed your fish several times during the day with measured and minimal feedings as opposed to one heavy feeding. That's the normal practice but you still have to consider the species of your fish.

For example, the popular blue-green chromis fish wants small feedings that are distributed throughout the day. Meanwhile, bigger predatory fish species like groupers and lionfish only need to be fed every other day.

Which is better? Live food or prepared food?

Live food seems like the no-brainer answer but it's not as simple as that. Pet shops rarely sell live fish food so you are often left with no other choice but to use prepared food.

I would still recommend using prepared food because it's much more convenient. And manufacturers of prepared fish food are getting better in hitting the right nutritional balance for various saltwater fish species.

Experienced fish owners often advise that the food you offer during a feeding session can be consumed by the fish within five minutes. If it takes them more than five minutes to clear away the food, that means you are feeding them too much.

In calculating the feeding time, you take into account the size of the tank and the number of saltwater fish contained in it.

Make sure that the bottom fish dwellers and invertebrates are well-fed as well. Don't ever assume that all fish feed near the surface or in the middle of the tank.

There are specific types of fish food in tablets or pellets that sink to the bottom of the tank.

Don't overfeed your fish. Overeating is one of the reasons why fish get stressed out.

It can also lead to the accumulation of detritus inside the tank which in turn degrades the quality of the water.

Feed your fish at the same spot in the tank. This is necessary if your tank contains both surface feeders and bottom feeders.

As the surface feeders are distracted and busy feeding, you can sneak in food down to the bottom feeders.

These practical tips should be more than enough to provide you with the information you need on the "hows" and "whens" of feeding saltwater fish in a tank. I know, feeding saltwater fish seems like a daunting and confusing task but it's only during the beginning.

The task gets simpler and easier as you learn more about the food requirements and feeding habits of every fish species you have.

Chapter Six: How to Properly Clean and Maintain a Saltwater Tank

Not regularly cleaning your tank is one of the worst mistakes you can make. Remember the nitrogen cycle that we discussed earlier?

If you don't clean your tank, that cycle gets broken and leads to the accumulation of toxic wastes inside the tank. The fish and other organisms inside the tank will eventually start dying out.

You should create a schedule on how and when you are going to clean your tank. Of course, your cleaning schedule will depend on several factors like the size of the tank and the number of fish that are inside it.

The general rule is that the more fish a tank contains, the more frequent your cleaning schedule should be.

Cleaning a saltwater tank is not that difficult or sophisticated. It's easy and it will take just a few minutes of your time.

Usually, it just involves changing the water and scrubbing the walls and floor of the aquarium to get rid of the accumulated wastes.

Aside from regularly cleaning the aquarium, you should also consider buying species of fish that are considered as "cleaning species" or "cleaners". In the simplest of terms, these are fish that help in cleaning the aquarium by removing external parasites and dead tissues.

The most common cleaner fish include the neon goby and the skunk cleaner shrimp. These are very helpful in keeping the tank clean.

However, you shouldn't rely on these cleaner fishes when it comes to cleaning duties. You still have to regularly clean the tank yourself.

The cleaner fish are there to assist you, not to take over your cleaning responsibilities.

I should also point out here that cleaning a tank doesn't mean you completely clean it out and scrub everything out. This isn't a good practice for the simple reason that the tank also contains bacteria that are beneficial to the health of the fish and critters.

Just think of these bacteria as very similar to the beneficial bacteria that are present in the guts of humans. These bacteria help the human stomach in digesting and extracting nutrients from the food we eat.

The same principle applies to the bacteria present inside a saltwater tank. When cleaning your saltwater tank, don't completely remove all of the water, substrate, and inhabitants in order to scrub it out.

There are several methods on how to clean a saltwater tank. In this chapter, we are going to look into some of these methods.

1. Remove Uneaten Food

The general rule is that you should only give your fish food that they can all consume during a feeding session. However, there will always be instances where there will be leftovers.

You can't leave these leftovers floating in the water because they can contaminate the tank, make it cloudy, or even mess up the nitrogen cycle. Whenever there's leftover food during a feeding session, use a small net to skim the leftovers out of the tank.

2. Remove 10% of the Water Every Two Weeks

It's advisable that you remove 10% of the tank's water and replace it every other two weeks. Use a siphon to slowly remove 10% of the water.

You can also use this opportunity to clean out the tank's pumps, hoses, and filters. Clean these up before you start adding new saltwater into the tank.

3. Cleaning the Glass Panes of the Tank

There are several reasons why the glass panes (both inside and outside) need to be cleaned on a regular basis. Bacteria can accumulate on the panes.

Algae can also grow on the panes. To clean the panes, you can use an algae sponge.

This will require you to stick your hands into the tank. If you want to avoid that, you can use a magnetic algae sponge which will allow you to guide the sponge from the outside of the tank.

When cleaner the outside glass panes you can use any sort of soft sponge or cleaner wipes. You don't want to use any sort of material that might scratch the glass of your tank.

Finally, make sure no cleaning chemicals or soaps get inside the tank when you're cleaning the outside of it!

4. Vacuum the Tank's Substrate When You Change the Water

The substrate is where the wastes, uneaten food, bad bacteria, and detritus accumulate. To clean it effectively, you should use a vacuum specifically designed for aquariums.

You can purchase these vacuums in pet supply shops. The vacuum uses a pump to suck out waste, algae overgrowth, and detritus from the substrate.

5. Wash and Rinse the Filters Regularly

Dirt and organisms can clog the filters if these aren't cleaned regularly. It's suggested that you do this every two weeks.

The good news is that you can turn off the filters for a while so that you can remove them and have them thoroughly washed and cleaned before being reinstalled.

Practical Tips in Maintaining the Saltwater Tank

-Always see to it that the tank's temperature is between 73 and 82 degrees Fahrenheit. These are the temperatures where saltwater fish thrive.

-Make sure that the water in the tank has the proper salinity. Salinity is measured in parts per one thousand units of water.

In context, the salinity of most oceans is around 34 to 37 parts per one thousand units of water. This is the salinity level you should have in your tank.

You can measure your tank's salinity using a hydrometer or refractometer. These can be bought in most pet supply stores. Most pet stores will even test this for free if you bring in a sample of your water.

-See to it that the tank has the appropriate pH level. This is basically a measurement pertaining to the amount of alkali or acid present in the water.

To measure the water's pH level, you can use color-coded testing strips which you can buy in most pet supply stores, or take a sample of your water to the pet store. The ideal pH level for a saltwater aquarium is between 8.0 and 8.4.

If the pH level is below 7.8 or above 8.5, then there is something wrong. You can increase the level by putting additives such as limewater into the tank.

You can also try growing microalgae in the tank.

-Keep the tank lights on for ten to twelve hours a day. Experts say that leaving the lights on will encourage the growth of beneficial bacteria which are helpful in speeding up the nitrogen cycle.

If you want your saltwater aquarium clean and functioning at all times, you should follow all the cleaning and maintenance tips discussed above. Not following these tips can cause all sorts of problems to your tank and its occupants.

Chapter Seven: Everything You Should Know About Saltwater Fish Illnesses and How to Treat Them

Fish contained in a saltwater tank are not immune to diseases regardless of how clean the tank is. There are a lot of reasons why a fish can acquire a certain illness. It could be caused by a number of things including:

- The food it eats.
- By toxic waste inside the tank.
- The disease could be transferred by new arrivals in the tank.
- It could be caused by a diseased sea critter such as a snail.

In short, there are many ways a fish can get ill. It's your responsibility to spot signs of an illness and address it immediately before it gets any worse or before the illness transfers to other occupants of the tank.

Before you add new fish inside a tank, it's common practice to quarantine them first before dumping them into the tank. This is very important because the new fish may be carrying diseases that can be transferred to the original occupants of the tank.

After purchasing the live fish from the store, you need to bring it home as soon as possible.

For good measure, you should consider adding a good amount of ammonia neutralizer in the bag or container carrying the fish. The ammonia neutralizer helps in dealing with the accumulated ammonia during transit.

This is very important if there are hours between buying the fish and you taking them home. Ammonia can easily build up during those few hours considering the fact that there's no filter in the bag.

Here's an overview of the most common symptoms for illnesses in saltwater fish:

No appetite. - If your fish just refuses to eat, there is something wrong. This is probably the most common symptom of fish illness.

Their appetite is the first thing to go if they are not healthy. When a fish is first introduced into a tank, it's not that unusual for the fish to not eat for a day or two because it's still adapting to the new environment.

But if it still refuses to eat for several more days, something is definitely wrong and you must have the fish checked out. Sometimes, the problem isn't with the fish but a problem with the tank so have the tank checked out as well.

White dots or a white powdery look on a fish's skin or fins. – In most cases, these white dots and powdery look occurs when the fish is infested by a marine parasite. The fish can be in serious danger because the parasites can grow to a critical number and subdue the fish's immune system.

These dots can be caused by one of the following: anemone fish disease, Brooklynella, Brooklynellosis, coral reef fish disease, marine velvet, Oodinium, Ichthyophthirius multifilis, marine white spot disease, or Cryptocaryon.

As you can see, there are several reasons why white dots are appearing on the skin or fins of your fish. Each of these illnesses requires different treatment procedures.

It's important that the correct disease is identified first so that you can come up with the proper treatment procedure. Take note of the following:

Popeye – This is a term often used to describe an eye that is enlarged and is protruding more than what's considered as normal from its socket. Eyes don't just protrude like this if there isn't a problem.

In most cases, popeye results from an infection that originates from within the eye itself. It's possible that the eye was injured, scratched, or affected by an abrasion.

What happens is that the injured portion of the eye gets infected by the bacteria in the water. The eye then bloats causing it to protrude from the eye socket.

Because popeye is caused by an infection to an injured eye, it usually occurs in just a single eye. One eye has the popeye while the other one looks good and healthy.

In instances where both eyes are enlarged and protruding, the illness is probably not just on one single eye but on the fish as a whole.

Cloudy eyes – Cloudy eyes are often signs of bacterial infection. It can be an injury to the eye or on any part of the fish.

You might be wondering how an injury on another part of the fish's body can cause cloudiness in the eyes. Well, during bacterial infections, bacteria enter the body and can travel all the way to the eyes.

For example, the fish's tail gets injured and the bacterial infection sets in. This infection does not just affect the tail of the fish, it travels through the fish's body.

The bacteria can definitely migrate all the way to the eyes of the fish. Thus resulting in the cloudiness that you might be observing.

We have discussed in an earlier chapter that some bacteria can be beneficial to the well-being of the fish inside the tank. However, too much bacteria is not a good thing.

Blooming bacteria can overrun even the healthiest of fish. This is why it's important that you regularly clean the tank to ensure that there is always a balance between good and bad bacteria.

Frayed fins – Fins do not just fray on their own. There are two common reasons why frayed fins occur.

One, there's an infection on the fins or on another part of the fish. And two, the frayed fins were caused by what is referred to as an ammonia burn.

Accumulated ammonia in the tank literally burns the edges of the fins. This occurs if the nitrogen cycle isn't properly being followed in the maintenance of the tank.

Ammonia is a very strong chemical. If it can literally burn the edges of the fins, it can also cause all sorts of problems on other parts of the fish.

To treat frayed fins, you should regularly clean the tank and address the fins like a usual infection problem.

Rapid gilling – Rapid gilling is characterized by breathing rapidly. This is an obvious sign that the fish isn't able to pump enough oxygen into its system.

Lack of oxygen can lead to more serious problems for the fish if it's not addressed immediately. Suffocation can occur if rapid gilling continues for long periods of time.

There are a few reasons why this problem may occur. One, it's possible that the water in the tank is so unclean that it's very difficult for the fish to get the correct amount of oxygen that it needs.

If this is the case, all you need to do is clean the tank, make sure that the filters are working, and see to it that there's proper air/water regulation inside the tank.

Another possible cause of rapid gilling is that the gills may have been clogged by mucus. Naturally, if the gills are clogged, the fish has to double its efforts in trying to bring in oxygen.

Parasites in the gills are often the culprits for the accumulation of mucus. Parasites irritate the gills to the point that the fish's immune system has to produce more mucus to protect itself. More mucus means less oxygen coming in.

Rapid gilling can also be caused by the over-abundance of ammonia in the water. Most saltwater fish can tolerate even beyond average levels of ammonia but if the ammonia level is too high, it can burn the gills.

Needless to say, this inhibits the fish's ability to take in oxygen. A common indication of high levels of ammonia in the water is the fraying of a fish's fin.

Open sores – These are raw spots that suddenly or gradually appear on the skin of a fish. These are frequently caused by parasites.

Parasites would attach themselves to the skin of the fish causing abrasions and irritations. These abrasions then get infected by bacteria and other microorganisms present in the water.

Open sores should be addressed immediately before they get any bigger.

Red fins – Something is wrong if you notice reddish colors on the fins of a fish. This usually indicates that there's a bacterial infection.

Bacteria have entered the body of the fish and have spread to its fins. As is always the case, bacteria often enter the body of the fish through abrasions and open sores created by ammonia burns.

It's quite easy for bacteria to enter the fish's skin and quickly spread to other parts of its body.

Faded colors – The fading of colors is often a sign that a fish is not that healthy. It's possible that the fish is stressed out or it's suffering from an illness.

Whatever the case may be, it must be addressed immediately before the situation gets any worse. The fading of colors does not necessarily mean that there's a change in colors.

It's possible for the fish to maintain the colors but it's still noticeable that the skin has lost its glint or luster.

However, it's worth mentioning here that there are certain types of saltwater fish that regularly change their colors as natural bodily mechanisms. There are various reasons why they do this.

It could be to protect themselves from potential predators. It could be a way of luring prey and food.

It could also be a courting tactic. You should also keep in mind that certain species of saltwater fish change colors depending on whether it's night or day.

You should be aware of these to prevent the risks of misdiagnosing illnesses in your fish.

Bloating or abdominal swelling – If the lower half of the fish's body seems enlarged, it could be due to abdominal swelling or bloating. A lot of people often make the wrong assumption that this bloating is due to eating too much.

But the reality is that it can still happen if the fish isn't eating that much food. Abdominal swelling and bloating are usually indications of an infection in the fish's bladder.

This is a major problem among wrasses because these types of fish love to burrow in the tank's substrate where there's usually a large concentration of harmful bacteria.

Scratching on rocks or corals – Sometimes, you will see your fish constantly scratching or rubbing itself on objects inside the tank. If this isn't a habit inherent in the fish species, then it is a clear indication that there's something amiss.

The most probable explanation is that the fish is suffering from irritations on its skin. It's rubbing its body in an attempt to remove the irritating material.

The irritating material can either be parasites or cysts caused by marine white spot disease or coral reef fish disease.

Now that you are aware of the most common symptoms in diseased saltwater fish, let's take a look into what these diseases really are and how they can be treated properly. Most fish illnesses are treatable without you taking the fish to a vet.

The key lies on properly categorizing the disease and determining its cause. If you are able to do these, then you can come up with the proper treatment procedure.

Common fish illnesses and their corresponding treatment options are discussed below.

Ammonia Poisoning – Here's what you need to understand. Too much ammonia in the water is bad for your saltwater fish.

There are two major signs of ammonia poisoning. One, the gills of the fish are uncharacteristically red or inflamed.

Two, the fish is constantly swimming to the surface gasping for air.

To fix this problem, you have to make sure that the tank is clean and that it has cycled. Ammonia can easily accumulate if the nitrogen cycle isn't properly being followed.

Frequent water changes have to be done to keep the ammonia levels down. You can also consider putting a substance called zeolite into the water.

This chemical helps a lot in absorbing ammonia in the water. Also, see to it that the tank isn't overcrowded because overcrowding is a major cause of ammonia accumulation.

Bacterial Infection – Bacterial infection is a major concern in saltwater fish. A huge percentage of saltwater fish problems are due to bacterial infection.

This is due to the fact that unmoving water in a tank is the perfect breeding ground for bacteria. There are several symptoms of bacterial infection.

These include bloated stomachs, raised, scaled, or frayed fins, inflamed gills, rapid gilling, enlarged eyes, white spots in the skin, and cloudy eyes.

The first thing you should do is improve the quality of the water by performing a 25% water change. You can't perform a complete water change especially if the water hasn't cycled yet.

I'm referring to the nitrogen cycle here. Try performing a 25% water change once every three days.

Observe closely if the condition of the fish improves. If it does not improve, the problem is serious and you need to resort to medication.

This usually involves dumping the medication right into the water or mixing the medication with the fish food. Before adding the medication, try removing the carbon filter inside the tank because this filter may absorb the medication.

Head and Lateral Line Erosion (HLLE) – This condition is sometimes referred to as Hole in the Head (HITH). This illness is characterized by tiny holes or small indentations and lines on the head of the fish.

If the condition is advanced, markings can also be observed along the lateral lines of the fish. The bad news is that very little is known about this condition or what causes it.

There are several theories but there's not enough scientific evidence to back them up.

However, it's commonly believed that HLLE and HITH are possibly caused by three things. These are often attributed to a lack of proper nutrition, poor water quality, and the use of activated carbon for long periods of time.

Logic dictates that you would address these issues if you wish to treat your fish suffering from HLLE or HITH. First of all, you need to perform frequent water changes to keep the water clean.

Give your fish vitamin-enriched food and supplements. Last but not least, rinse thoroughly the activated carbon filters that you are using in your tank's filtration system.

Or you can try deactivating the carbon filters altogether and see what happens. If the health of the fish improves immediately after the removal of carbon filters, then the filters are potentially the culprit for the fish's illness.

Marine Ich (Also referred to as ick or cryptocaryon) –This is one of the most common illnesses in fish contained in a tank. However, it is easily treatable if caught in the early stages.

It's mostly caused by parasites attaching themselves to the fish. Before you introduce a fish into a saltwater tank where there's already fish in it, quarantine the new fish first before putting it into the tank.

Marine ich can also be caused by stress and we all know that fish get stressed when introduced to a brand new environment. Quarantining the fish first should help a little in addressing this problem.

Symptoms of marine ich include white spots suddenly appearing on the fins or skin of the fish. Sometimes, it looks like someone dribbled rock salt all over the fish because of the white spots.

Another common symptom is the fish develops the habit of rubbing itself on objects within the tank.

As for treatment, you have several options. Your best option is to use medication. Medication for marine ich can be bought in most pet stores.

You can also buy the medication online if there isn't a pet store near your location. As always, remove the tank's carbon filters before adding the medication into the water because the carbon filters may absorb the medication.

Another treatment procedure you can apply involves increasing the temperature in the water to 82 degrees

Fahrenheit. Some believe that this speeds up the cycle time of parasites.

Most saltwater fish don't have any problems with temperatures of up to 82 degrees Fahrenheit. So this treatment method is worth trying. Just make sure that you steadily increase the temperature instead of making one big jump to 82 degrees.

You want to give your fish time to accumulate to the increasing temperature.

Nitrite or Nitrate Poisoning – Technically speaking, nitrite or nitrate poisoning is not a disease. Complicating the matter even worse is the fact that it's often difficult to pinpoint nitrite and nitrate poisoning.

Symptoms of this condition include lethargy and drowsiness in the fish. If your fish is usually active inside the tank but then it suddenly looks lazy, chances are it's suffering from either nitrite or nitrate poisoning.

Another symptom of this condition is the fish often resting just below the surface of the water.

So far, the most effective way to identify nitrite or nitrate poisoning is to make use of a nitrate test kit. This kit enables you to measure the levels of nitrite and nitrate in the water.

If you are getting high readings and the fish are displaying the symptoms I mentioned earlier, then they are more than likely suffering from nitrite or nitrate poisoning.

After identifying nitrate poisoning, you should perform a partial water change immediately. Do more partial water changes.

All the while, you should monitor the levels of nitrate in the water using a nitrate test kit. The water changes should be able to lower the nitrate to a healthy and manageable level.

After reaching a stable level, review why the nitrate level in the tank rose to such a dangerous level. Maybe you're not cleaning the tank as regularly as you should.

Maybe there are too many fish inside the tank. Or maybe the nitrogen cycle isn't going properly.

Address these issues to prevent further nitrate poisoning in the future. And keep using the nitrate test kit to ensure that nitrate levels inside the tank don't go beyond what's considered as normal levels.

Oxygen Starvation – Saltwater fish need a steady supply of oxygen to survive. Oxygen starvation happens if the fish can't get enough oxygen from the tank.

There are two major indications that there's oxygen starvation among your fish. One, most if not all of the fish tend to be hanging out near the surface of the water.

Two, they often gulp at the surface with their mouths wide open. If these happen, especially at the same time, then there's an obvious lack of oxygen in your tank.

The first thing you should do is increase the aeration inside the tank. You can do this by adding air stones.

You can also increase the water flow rate by ramping up your filters. Sometimes, doing these things won't be enough to get more oxygen circulating in the water.

This is because the oxygen starvation may be caused by something else. For example, the temperature inside the tank may have gone too high.

High water temperatures require higher levels of oxygen. So what you need to do is check the temperature inside the tank.

If the temperature is higher than normal, you should address it immediately. Try decreasing the temperature by putting ice cubes in a sealed plastic bag then have it float inside the tank.

Turn off the tank's lights as well. If sunlight is entering the tank, close the windows and the shades. In a nutshell, lowering the water temperature and increasing aeration and flow rate in the tank should be able to fix the problem of oxygen starvation among the fish.

Marine Velvet or Oodinium (also referred to as Coral Reef Fish Disease) – This is an illness that people often confuse with marine ich. That's not surprising given the fact that the two are very similar with regards to their symptoms.

However, there's a slight difference in the symptoms. The white dots caused by velvet are smaller.

Sometimes, these are gray dusty spots and not white spots. Fish that have velvet often display rapid gill movement.

They also tend to keep rubbing themselves on objects inside the tank.

The most effective way to treat this disease is through medication. There are several medications that you can use.

Just go to your nearest pet store and ask for something that you can use to treat velvet in fish. One of the most popular medications for velvet is a product called Aquarisol.

What's great about this product is that it can also be used to treat machine ich. So if you are not sure whether your fish is afflicted by marine ich or velvet, it really doesn't matter because the medication is basically the same.

Just mix the Aquarisol in the water and you are good to go.

Anemone Fish Disease or Brooklynellosis – This is caused by a parasite called the ciliated protozoa. This parasite infects the gills or skin of the fish. Signs and symptoms of Brooklynellosis include increased secretion of mucus, sloughing of the epithelium, lethargy, decreased appetite, discoloring of the skin, and respiratory distress.

The parasite attaches itself on the fish and feeds on the fish's tissue and blood. This disease often afflicts anemone fish (thus the name) but it can also affect other saltwater fish species (i.e. seahorses).

The most common way to treat anemone fish disease is to use a mixture of malachite green and formalin. However, when using formalin, you have to be careful because it can poison fish with severely damaged skin.

As to malachite green, you should make use of a concentration of 0.10 ppm or slight variations like 0.9 or 0.11 ppm. Try to expose the fish to malachite green within one week or ten days.

Another effective treatment method involves significantly decreasing the water's salinity level. This helps in eradicating the stenohaline parasite.

This type of parasite can only tolerate a rather narrow range of salinity. Reducing salinity requires replacing the water in the tank.

But don't replace the water in one go. It's highly recommended that you replace only half of the water in the tank. And you should do this within a couple of hours.

Fish Tuberculosis or Wasting Disease – The main cause of this disease is the Mycobacterium bacteria. This is one of the most frustrating fish illnesses because it has very little external signs.

On the outside, the fish may look healthy and fine but inside of the fish, bacteria is quickly spreading and infecting its internal organs.

In rare instances, the fish may display external symptoms such as loss of appetite, frayed fins, scale loss, labored breathing, emaciation, and skin lesions. However, these are symptoms that are also associated with several other fish illnesses.

This means that the disease is often not diagnosed as fish tuberculosis. When this happens, the bacteria has already spread to the point that it's too late to try and save the fish.

In short, fish tuberculosis is treatable if it's diagnosed in its early stages.

The best treatment against fish tuberculosis is prevention. As I've mentioned above, when it's diagnosed as fish tuberculosis, it's already too late.

Infected fish usually live for less than a year after such a diagnosis. To prevent fish tuberculosis, you need to be aware of the ways it's transmitted.

It's usually transmitted when a fish ingests flesh, detritus, or feces coming from an already infected fish. The bacteria can also enter a fish's body through skin lesions, wounds, and abrasions. Infections occur almost instantly.

To minimize risks of fish tuberculosis, you should avoid feeding raw fish and shellfish to your saltwater fish. The flesh may be contaminated with the type of bacteria that causes the disease.

You can also consider using antibiotics like streptomycin, erythromycin, and kanamycin. If the disease is at its early stages, antibiotics can be effective in completely eradicating it.

If a fish in your tank dies from fish tuberculosis, you should clean the tank immediately. Discard the water and sterilize the tank before putting things back in.

Whirling Disease – This is an illness caused by the Ichthyophonus fungus. This is a type of fungus that's parasitic to saltwater fish.

What's scary about these parasites is that it's so easy for them to enter the fish's body. Fungal cysts floating in the water gets ingested by the fish.

These fungal cysts then burst open and make their way into the fish's bloodstream. Since they are in the bloodstream, they can infect every internal organ of the fish.

With that being said, a fish infected by this fungus typically dies two months after the occurrence of the infection. That's how quick the parasite kills its host.

Signs and symptoms of the whirling disease include erratic swimming behavior, skin ulcers, fin erosion, fin fraying, roughening of the skin, skin discoloration, spinal curvature, and body emaciation.

Treating whirling disease is very difficult because the infection involves nearly all of the fish's internal organs.

You can try medications like probiotic marine formula and rich ich but these rarely lead to full recovery.

They can prolong the life of the fish for a few days or weeks but that's just about it.

What you should do is remove the infected fish from the tank before it infects the other occupants. Then clean and replace the water because there's always the possibility that there are still fungi cysts floating in the water.

Trematode Infestation – This is a nasty disease that is caused by monogenetic trematode worms. These worms are sometimes too small that you are going to need a microscope to be able to see them.

They infest the fish through the mouth, skin, eyes, gills, and anal opening. They cause irritation and inflammation.

Infected fish rub themselves against objects inside the tank in an attempt to get rid of the parasites. To treat this illness, try medications like trichlorfon, praziquantel, and mebendazole.

You can also try immersing the fish in freshwater for a short period of time.

Lymphocystis or Cauliflower Disease – This disease is characterized by the formation of white bumps that suddenly form on the body of an infected fish. It's caused by a virus and it usually infects stressed fish in unclean tanks.

Because of the white spots, it's often misdiagnosed as marine ich. Unfortunately, there is no known cure for the cauliflower disease.

Your only option is to have it quarantined in another container before it infects other fish in the tank.

Some suggest euthanizing the fish and spare it from further suffering especially if the disease is at its final stages.

These are the most common saltwater diseases and symptoms. It's very important that you are aware of them so that you will be able to catch diseases earlier.

The earlier you diagnose a fish illness, the better chances you have of treating it and affording it a complete recovery.

Conclusion

The fact that you've made it to this point tells me that you are really serious about setting up your own saltwater aquarium. Well, congratulations!

The only thing left to do now is to get started. I've discussed all the major points in setting up and maintaining a saltwater tank throughout this book.

This information will help you set up a tank and it will help to ensure the well-being and survival of your marine creatures.

I've written this book not just as a guidebook for beginners but as a reference book as well. Be sure to return to it if you're encountering certain problems with your tank.

You might forget some things so it never hurts to go back over some of the information. Who knows you might even pick up on something you didn't realize the first time you read it!

Taking care of saltwater fish seems daunting at first because of how sensitive they are but it gets easier and more fun as you get used to the routine. You will learn a lot of things about how to take care of them along the way.

That means you'll get better in ensuring their survival with the passage of time. In other words, don't feel too bad about yourself if you make a lot of mistakes early on.

It happens to all of us. Making mistakes is normal among first-time saltwater aquarium owners.

Last but not least, I have one last favor to ask of you. Please share or recommend this book to anyone planning or interested in setting up his or her own saltwater aquarium.

That someone could be a family member, a close friend, a neighbor, or a colleague. Let this book help them the way it helped you.

Thank you very much for reading this book and good luck setting up your own saltwater aquarium. Have fun!

Did you enjoy reading this book? If so, please consdier leaving a review. Even just a few words would help others decide if the book is right for them.

Best regards and thanks in advance—Anthony Daniels

Made in the USA
Monee, IL
27 June 2025

20092842R00037